SELF LOVE
POETRY
For Thinkers & Feelers

MELODY GODFRED,
The Self Love Philosopher

Andrews McMeel
PUBLISHING®

Andrews McMeel Publishing
a division of Andrews McMeel Universal
1130 Walnut Street, Kansas City, Missouri 64106

www.andrewsmcmeel.com

23 24 25 26 27 VEP 10 9 8 7 6

ISBN: 978-1-5248-7122-2

Library of Congress Control Number: 2021941275

Editor: Patty Rice
Art Director: Julie Barnes
Production Editor: Jasmine Lim
Production Manager: Cliff Koehler

ATTENTION: SCHOOLS AND BUSINESSES
Andrews McMeel books are available at quantity discounts with
bulk purchase for educational, business, or sales promotional use.
For information, please e-mail the Andrews McMeel Publishing
Special Sales Department: sales@amuniversal.com.

DEDICATION

"My life has suddenly awoken with such a jolt that I think I'll be awake forever."
—Melody, age 11

Dedicated to my childhood self: a thoughtful, heart-forward girl who wrote poetry to make sense of her outer and inner worlds.

Melody, we did it. We did it!

ACKNOWLEDGMENTS

I couldn't have written this book without my self love community on Instagram (@fredandfar). Thank you for showing up for me each day, reading my poetry, sharing it, and embodying everything it stands for. You inspire my words every day.

I'm also deeply grateful to Paige Feldman, Leanne Aranador, Erin Hosier, and Patty Rice. Without them, this book would still simply be my childhood dream.

As you'll see in these poems, my family is a constant source of inspiration. Thank you to my husband Aaron, daughters Stella and Violet, son Teddy, my parents, and all the family and friends who have read my poetry and supported my writing over the past thirty years.

INTRODUCTION

Writing a book of poetry has been one of my biggest dreams. But when the time came to review my poetry for inclusion in a book, I found myself at a standstill: how do I reconcile all 700 pieces so they make sense as a book? You see, my poetry doesn't follow one singular style. It's a reflection of whatever I'm feeling at any given moment. Sometimes, that's a gut-punch of a sentence, and sometimes it's a long, sensory experience filled with lush words and imagery.

It wasn't until I was willing to embrace this duality within myself that the concept for this book came to life: 100 pairs of poems, each with a central theme. The left page for left-brain thinkers, the right page for right-brain feelers. Each pair of poems is in conversation and works in tandem to activate the whole brain experience in all of us. The result is a book of poetry that I am so deeply proud and excited to share with you.

As you read these poems, please let them be a reminder: it's only when you embrace all parts of yourself that your authentic self can work her magic and enable you to make the impact on the world <u>only you</u> were born to make. I believe this book is mine.

SELF LOVE POETRY
For Thinkers & Feelers

LEFT BRAIN
(THINKERS)

RIGHT BRAIN
(FEELERS)

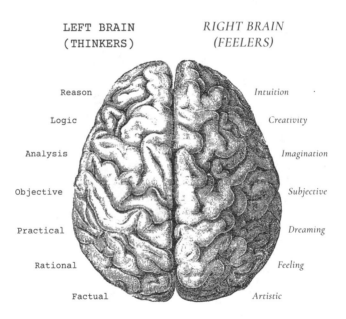

Reason

Logic

Analysis

Objective

Practical

Rational

Factual

Intuition

Creativity

Imagination

Subjective

Dreaming

Feeling

Artistic

Once you can accept that
the thing you want most
might not happen, you can
also accept that it just
might happen, too.

And either way,
you will be okay.

I thought I knew,
and then I KNEW.
I thought I loved,
and then I LOVED.
I thought I surrendered,
and then I SURRENDERED.
I thought it was over,
and then it BEGAN.

I thought this would be
the year I get
everything I want.

Now I know this is
the year I appreciate
everything I have.

Expectation closed my eyes.
Gratitude opened them.
Fear closed my eyes.
Trust opened them.
Complaining closed my eyes.
Appreciation opened them.
Perfection closed my eyes.
Authenticity opened them.
Guilt closed my eyes.
Self love opened them.

If putting everyone
else's needs first
hasn't worked,
there is another option . . .

*Choosing yourself
might be the hardest decision
you ever make because
guilt, shame, and fear
are powerful gatekeepers.*

*Do it anyway.
You are more powerful
than they are.
Much more.*

Everything can change, and
I will still be joyful.

Nothing can change, and
I will still be joyful.

Under the
dust of disappointment
weight of responsibility
ache of pain
tremor of doubt
numb of fear, and
burn of resentment . . .
Your true self remains.
She is light, fluid, free,
soft, and steady.
Her joy untethered from
what has been or what will be.

If your hard work
feels unseen,
stop making it
look so effortless.

We wake up early.
We exercise. We eat well.
We work on healing our trauma. We smile.
We drink water. We water our plants.
We make time to volunteer.
We excel at work. We excel as parents.
As aunts. As friends. As caretakers.
We work on our desire.
We live by gratitude and die by kindness.
We make eye contact. We limit our screen time.
We look damn good. We moisturize. We exfoliate.
We manicure our nails and tame our hair.
We smell good. We read books. We make time for
people in need. We host dinner parties. We remember
birthdays—and birthday gifts. We start the company.
We take care of the pets. We research the ingredients.
We plan the vacations. We never complain.
We wake up. We do it again.
We clock in. We never clock out.
We make it look easy. We make it look easy.
We make it look easy.
(It wasn't. It isn't. It never will be.)

Choosing yourself doesn't
make self care easier.
It takes WORK to show up
for yourself every day.

But it does make
sacrificing, neglecting,
doubting, and compromising
yourself harder.

You simply won't
settle for that anymore.

A powerful woman lives
not at the surface
but in her depths.
She makes her bed among
the roots of her being.

She is at home in her light
and at peace with her darkness.
She listens when her intuition speaks
and doesn't react when her ego screams.

She reflects in her moments of stillness;
she rises in her moments of clarity.

She appears as she is:
whole, worthy, abundant,
purposed, divine, chosen.

Hey you. Yes, you.
All of you. Yes, all of you.
Every piece of you.
Every second of your story.
Every inch of your body.
Every branch of your history.
Every corner of your mind.
Is worthy of deep, unwavering,
soul-shaking, home-feeling love.

Got it?

Your highs. Your lows.
Your power. Your vulnerability.
Your voice. Your silence.
Your shape. Your light.
Your patience. Your momentum.
Your joy. Your despair.
Your playfulness. Your gravity.
Your hands. Your brain.
Your grace. Your neuroses.
Your forgiveness. Your fire.
Your flaws. Your perfection.
Your desires. Your acceptance.
Your might. Your softness.
Your courage. Your anxiety.
Your mess. Your magnitude.
Your jokes. Your anger.
Your hugs. Your tears.
Your integrity. Your ingenuity.
Your talent. Your conviction.
Your vision. Your resilience.
All of you. That's what I love.

When I started approving
my own choices,
guilt and shame became
powerless over me.

*She owned her choices
and her moods
both high and low.
Her happiness
was hers to cultivate.
She was the cause,
the catalyst.
She was her own.*

I let go of my expectations and
stopped feeling disappointed.

I stopped feeling disappointed and
started feeling alive.

I didn't realize how much I was carrying until I put it all down.

New dreams take time.
If the door has closed
on the future
you thought you'd live,
give yourself time to
dream up a new one.

Learn to speak your dreams.
Let them spill onto pages.
Fill up quiet rooms.
Taste your dreams
as they roll around in your mouth,
awakening dormant taste buds
like the first berries of summer.
Know them, inside out and outside in,
dreams so vivid you can hear them.
A steady hum of hope in your ears.

Negative thought:
I believed it so deeply
it became real.

Positive thought:
I believed it so deeply
it became real.

Your choice.

When good things happen,
I catch myself holding my breath.
Anxiously waiting for it to go wrong, for them to vanish.
Like a mirage that was never really real to begin with.
Even my kids. I look at them and think,
"I can't believe you're real. I can't believe you're mine."

I don't feel this way about my worries. They are real.
They are so real, in fact, that at night they
enter the room and lie beside me,
as real as the pillow under my head.

My fears, anxiety, pain, doubt, guilt.
These are the things I never question.
I never say, "I can't believe you're real.
I can't believe you're mine."
I own them and wear them like a uniform.

But no more. Starting today, I will believe
my blessings instead of my fears.
I will look at my blessings and say,
"You are real. You are mine."
And when my worries try to visit me tonight,
I will say,
"I don't believe you are real.
I don't believe you are mine."
And my blessings and I will rest.

The feeling you get
when you start listening
to your inner voice
instead of shushing it.

Remember how it felt to
start something new,
to feel yourself growing,
learning, becoming
stronger, sharper,
more powerful.

Remember thinking,
"How did I even live before?"
The newness so deeply
embedded in the very
essence of who you are.

Consider that while you
may now feel life is
monotonous, dull, a hum
of repeated tasks and emotions,
that potential for experiencing the
exhilaration of newness
is still within you . . .
all you have to do is
claim it.

Where your intuition
leads, the entire
universe follows.
Trust her.

My ME creates space
for the unknown.
She can remember the past
without being defined by it.
She can manifest the future
without being tied to it.
She is present.
She is peaceful.
She is powerful.

Sometimes just when you think
you have it all figured out,
it all falls apart.

This isn't a test;
you weren't naïve.
Life isn't linear.
Blessings aren't linear.
Progress isn't linear.

All is not lost;
you're still on your way.

Keep going.

*I finally
found my rhythm
when I realized
that even
the steps backward
were part
of the dance.*

When I can't move my mind,
I move my body.

When I can't move my body,
I move my mind.

Either way,
movement heals.

If you feel stuck, move.
Move your energy around.
Through dance.
Through conversation with
someone who needs
to hear your truth.
Through honest words
written on a page.
Through fingers passing
through an ocean wave
or planting in the dirt.
Move until your energy
feels free. Unstuck.
Vibrant. Resplendent.
Powerful. Holy. Alive.

Open. Your. Eyes.

Opportunity abounded.
The air ripe with hope.
My throat coated with the
buzz of possibility.

But I couldn't see them.
The round peaches just
within my reach on
branches heavy with
emerald leaves.

My eyes glazed over with
guilt, my fists tense
with regret, my lips
pursed in defense, and my
cheeks flushed with shame.

The fruit turning to rot.
The sweet smell of summer
now making me sick.
So much presence lost
because my body was here,
but my mind was not.

Loving yourself first
doesn't mean
loving anyone else less.

I belong to me,
you belong to you,
let's belong to ourselves,
together.

We've tried
giving ourselves less.

Isn't it time we try
giving ourselves more?

Today, give yourself
permission.
No, more than that.
Give yourself everything.
All of it.
Time, the benefit of the doubt,
gifts, patience, affirmation,
the extra mile,
delightful surprises,
validation, trust,
a soft touch, smiles,
forgiveness, faith,
unconditional love.

All the things once
reserved for our lovers,
for our children . . .
Take them.
They are yours.

My wish for you:

to be alone without being lonely
to reflect without regret
to anticipate without fear
to love without dependence
to give without expectation
to grow without attachment
to embrace yourself without exception
to be here now without distraction
to live joyfully without condition
to choose yourself without
guilt, shame,
doubt, or hesitation.

If anger sets you on fire,
let self love be your water.

If shame suffocates you,
let self love be your air.

If doubt paralyzes you,
let self love be your catalyst.

If fear isolates you,
let self love be your companion.

If anxiety attacks you,
let self love be your defense.

If depression clouds you,
let self love be your light.

If regret chains you,
let self love set you free.

When there is a choice,
claim it and take action.

When there is no choice,
claim that too,
through surrender
instead of resistance.

Surrender:
Ended the race.
Won the war.
Slowed the pace.
Claimed the present.
Took the breath.
Felt the feelings.
Healed the wound.
Quieted the mind.
Opened the heart.
Paved the way.

Your worth isn't their choice.
It's yours.

*The moment
I untethered my worth
from my ability to
generate dollar signs,
clicks, follows, and likes,
I realized my abundance
is priceless and
cannot be quantified.*

WARNING!

Common side effects of
self love include losing
the weight of guilt,
shame, doubt, fear, and
toxic relationships.

Fear of confrontation used to silence me.
Self love raised my voice.
Fear of failure used to immobilize me.
Self love emboldened me.
Fear of judgment used to consume me.
Self love made me whole.
Fear of abandonment used to anchor me.
Self love helped me set sail.

When you realize
you're the "one,"
life becomes
less about searching
and more about living.

When you feel most invisible,
I will see you.
When you feel most unlovable,
I will love you.
When you feel most proud,
I will celebrate you.
When you feel most alone,
I will accompany you.
When you feel most excited,
I will revel with you.
When you feel most uncomfortable,
I will comfort you.
When you feel most emotional,
I will feel with you.
When you feel most lost,
I will remind you of you.
When you feel most you,
I will be one with you.

—note to self

Start replacing
the question marks
in your mind with
exclamation points.

What if?

What if!

You are born with a superpower:

It's your imagination. Your ability to dream.
You can construct a vision for the future
beyond anything you've ever experienced.
Beyond what is currently even possible.

Knowing you have this gift, stop seeing only what is
missing from your life. Negativity dulls your
imagination and fuels your fear. It immobilizes.
It robs you of the color and juice of life.

See the color. Taste the juice.

Use your gift to dream up a world
we would all relish being a part of.
Then take action in service to your
dreams, and watch as the universe bends
in your favor to make them possible.

If life feels
impossible, remember:
if you change,
everything changes.

I felt stuck
so I embraced stillness.
I felt powerless
so I embraced surrender.
I felt emotional
so I embraced vulnerability.
I felt abandoned
so I embraced my own company.
I felt ashamed
so I embraced my story.
I felt empty
so I embraced
my authenticity
my wholeness
my worth.

Instead of warning each other,
"You can't change them."

We should remind each other,
"You can change yourself!"

I don't crave your power
because I am full of power.
I am powerfully me.
I am powerfully my own.

Of all the
things I own,
my worth is my
favorite possession.

I am mine:

To define.
To encourage.
To enlighten.
To adore.
To challenge.
To delight.
To accommodate.
To accept.
To welcome.
To love.

Sure.*
Okay.*
Fine.*

*Fake words we should
ban from our vocabularies
that actually mean
not okay, not at all.

Self love removes the dam
so your truth can flow freely.

Nothing will ever be
enough until you
decide it is enough.

Is it enough?
Are you enough?

It's up to you.

*I tried being
strong enough
smart enough
creative enough
bold enough
strategic enough
sexy enough
pretty enough
tough enough.*

*Only when I decided I was enough,
was I MORE than enough.*

If women didn't forget,
diminish, or dull their
pain, the human race would
cease to exist.

But if women forget,
diminish, or dull their
joy, the human race will
cease to exist, too.

Let me tell you about a woman's love:
It finds the cracks and fills them with light.
It sees the path and paves it.
It is both loud and quiet, strong and soft.
Patient, kind, and full—it is both
a realist and an optimist.
It holds a magic so powerful
that it is impossible to define
and can only be received and witnessed,
learned from and appreciated.

The best way
to cope with an
uncertain future
is to be
fully present.

*Enjoy your bliss without
worry or expectation.
Happiness is too delicate to
bear the weight of our fear.*

I started doing this "I Am" exercise
with my daughters. We go in a circle
and fill in the blank about ourselves.

At first, they kept gravitating to
"I like" instead of "I am."

And even I, someone who is diligently
trying to practice self love daily,
had a hard time.

What am I? I am creative. I am loving.
I am . . . I really had to search myself,
and I witnessed my daughters grappling
with it, too. One kept making a joke
of it. "I am goofy," and the other
would simply repeat my "I am" as hers.
So, we're going to keep at it. Because
self worth comes from self knowledge.
And we could all, at any age, stand to
get to know ourselves better.

When you have an arsenal of "I ams" ready,
it's easier to drown out the "I'm nots."
So for me, today, I am brave
because there's a lot of change and
uncertainty, and I'm calm, and my heart
is open to all of it.

What about you?

I AM BRAVE.
I AM CREATIVE.
I AM SMART.
I AM POWERFUL.
I AM RESILIENT.
I AM WHOLE.
I AM WORTHY.
I AM MAGIC.
I AM OPEN.
I AM FREE.
I AM ME.

If you want
something done right,
you have to do it ~~yourself.~~

with the help of
capable people who
deserve your trust.

Turning down help
is paying full price
for something that's on sale.

Letting go doesn't
mean you're losing.

I used to think if I was strong enough, I could handle
everything on my own. And you know what I realized?
"Strong" based on control is actually quite fragile.
Holding all the pieces together is impossible.
One wrong move and everything falls apart.
Now I aim to be soft. To be fluid, flexible, adaptable,
in harmony with my environment and those around
me, instead of in opposition. If strength used to come
from control for me, now it comes from softness.
From surrender. From letting go, leaning on those
around me, breathing in and breathing out, embracing
uncertainty, and enjoying my newfound grace.

This is the softness I speak of.
This is the softness that is supremely powerful,
unbreakable, eternal.
This is the softness that comes from self love.

You can't pour
from an empty cup,
but you can't drink
from an empty cup, either.

Pour the glass.
Drink the water.
You first.

I felt my feelings, and my heart said thank you.
I spoke my truth, and my mind said thank you.
I moved my energy, and my body said thank you.
And because I did, my world said thank you, too.

How to free your mind:

write down the things you
need to remember
for the future, and

write down the things you
need to let go of
from the past.

Open the windows,
let in the breeze,
and when you feel it
tickling your skin,
let it carry away
the endless to-dos,
the unforgiving should haves,
the perpetual buzz of thoughts
from past and future,
and replace them with the
smell of orange blossoms
in the spring.

The thing you are
avoiding is most likely
the key to you fully
claiming your worth.

Go there.

*If it's
uncomfortable,
say it
do it
leave it
heal it
sooner.*

Choose yourself.
Without explanation.
Without hesitation.
Without deliberation.
Without fear.
Without apology
or a disclaimer.

Do it fully.
Do it proudly.
Do it lovingly.
Do it unconditionally.
Do it now.

Realizing my potential
is not about conquering
the space between
where I am and
where I want to be.

It is about recognizing
that who I am
in every moment
is already enough.

I am not for everyone.
I am for me.

*The true learning has been
not just to love myself,
but to like myself.
To enjoy myself in the
mundane moments,
not just the sacred ones.*

Loving yourself isn't about being happy all the time. In fact, it's the opposite: it's about loving even your sadness. It's about claiming everything you've been through and everything you are—including your pain, your trauma, your mistakes, your wounds, your lowest lows, your shame, your regrets.

It's a love founded in integration and acceptance. When you can love it all, you will finally experience peace— within yourself and with your world.

Sometimes I'm a joyful
ray of sunshine.
Sometimes I'm a melancholy
beam of moonlight.
Happy or sad,
I am still whole,
I am still worthy,
I am still trying,
I am still enough,
I am still here,
I am still me.

Instead of learning
from the past
learn from your future:
plot your destiny
and align your
present with it.

The future used to live
on the edge of my memories,
a recipe passed down
for generations
lingering on my lips.

Now the future lives
not in my inheritance,
but in my desire,
as I shape the way
it will taste
with each breath.

The only way to get
where you're going
is to be where you are.

*I've decided to start
treating my daily life
like I treat travel:
taking it slow,
taking it all in,
and relishing every
sight, sound, touch,
breath, and taste.*

I used to feel like a boat,
completely at the mercy of
an ocean of thoughts that beat
against me one wave at a time.

Now I realize
I am not the boat.
I am the ocean.

I am the ocean.
I am the wave.
I am a single drop of water
that meets the shore.
I am as big
and as small
and as wild
and as calm
as I need to be
in every moment.

The conversation
you're afraid to have
is the one you need
to have the most.

Have it sooner.

Now is the time to:

say what needs to be said,
do what needs to be done,
heal what needs to be healed,
love what needs to be loved,
try what needs to be tried,
leave what needs to be left.

If you're in a bad mood,
have a headache,
feel lethargic,
can't remember anything,
are sensitive to pain,
and/or can't focus,
there is a very good chance
YOU ARE DEHYDRATED.

You can live without
self love, just like a
plant can live without
water, for a time.
But you will both grow
dry and brittle and gray.

We instantly forget our
happiness but memorize
our worries.

What would happen if we
did the opposite?

I'm made of trillions of cells.
I'm done letting one negative thought
make all of them suffer.

When you start
to doubt your resilience,
please consider that
our lives were
turned upside down,
and you're still here,
right side up.

Set the table for two.
Use your finest china.

Now tell me,
whom have you invited:
fear or love?

Want to experience
time travel?

Love yourself enough
to revisit old wounds
and heal them.

*When you can stand
naked before yourself,
stripped of guilt and shame,
anger and regret,
the woman you will see
is your authentic self.
Choose her.*

Give yourself
permission.
You know what you
need to do.

*Somewhere deep beneath
the wreckage caused by
heartbreak, fear, failure,
and responsibility is the
seed of curiosity that
fueled your first
years of life.*

*It craves what it has
always craved: an open
heart and unburdened mind
eager to live fully.*

*Water this seed within
you with self love and
watch yourself bloom
beyond the damage,
like a vine that won't stop
until it reaches the light.*

Together we will raise
a generation of
self-loving women.
Imagine the possibilities.

To teach them that
self love is sacred,
and self care is survival.
To show them that
they are born whole,
and all the love they need
is within their own hands.
To model for them what it means
for a woman to choose herself,
each and every day.
This is
my role
as a mother
of daughters.

It's not about
being single or
partnered.

It's about being
whole within
yourself either way.

*At first, I wore my heart
on my sleeve . . .
and so she belonged
to the world.*

*Then I wore my heart
in your hands . . .
and so she belonged
to you.*

*Now I wear my heart
in my chest . . .
and when she beats,
I remember that
she belongs to me.*

Everything is impermanent.
This is both
our greatest comfort,
and our greatest pain.

*Today I remember
that life is precious,
and what is here now
could be gone
a second from now.*

*Today I remember
that we are only safe
because we all agree to
live in harmony,
instead of harm.*

*Today I remember
that everyone can choose
to be brave, and
bravery saves lives.
Kindness does, too, especially
on days like today.*

*Today I remember.
Tomorrow I'll remember, too.*

Put on ~~a brave face.~~

any face that
represents
the way you're
actually feeling.

When things got hard,
I used to close
all my windows and doors,
my soul tucked away
in a quiet box.

Now I embrace
vulnerability—
windows open,
freedom abundant,
moonlight rushing in
to spotlight
my truth.

Reclaim the wholeness
you sacrificed to make
empty people feel full.

If I gave you more
than I had to give,
would you notice
the emptiness I swallowed
in exchange for your fullness?

A self-loving woman does
what she needs to do
to take care of herself.

Even if it's
uncomfortable.

Especially if it's
uncomfortable.

When I stopped
withholding from myself,
the nature of
my cravings changed
from intense indulgences
to healthy commitments.

It is as though my body
had simply been screaming
through extremes
for the constant
simplicity it
actually desired.

This space is for you.
Please use it.

I healed my fear
and made space for
my wonder.

I healed my anger
and made space for
my peace.

I healed my shame
and made space for
my love.

I healed my regret
and made space for
my joy.

Self love illuminates
your entire world with
the flame of one match.

I burned my guilt.
I burned my shame.
I burned my doubt.
I burned my regret.

And from the fire
of my self love,
I was born.

SELF CARE 101

1. Stop the 1,000 things you're doing.
2. Experience your feelings.
3. Create space for your needs.
4. Do something that meets them.

I wiped off my shame,
cleansed my expectations,
and watched as my anxiety
melted away.

I scrubbed my guilt and
applied healing tinctures
to alleviate my stress,
my trauma, my regret.

I poured a bath of my
love and soaked in it,
feeling it replenish me
from skin to soul.

Self care gets easier
with practice.
Self love gets easier
with practice.
Self worth gets easier
with practice.
Self discovery gets easier
with practice.

Life gets easier
with all of the above.

Self love isn't lust.
It isn't a fierce moment
of unbridled passion.
It's slow and tender.
A steady energetic hum
that fills you up
from head to toe.
And when you practice it,
it radiates off you,
full of life
and light
and magic.

Don't confuse
habits with comfort.
Just because it feels
familiar, doesn't mean
it's good for you.

I stopped feeling bruised
when I stopped
using myself
as a punching bag.

Your voice will
only be heard
if you use it.

Speak to yourself.
Speak to your loved ones.
Speak to your colleagues.
Speak to your representatives.
Speak to your world.

We are listening.

When you silence your needs,
your soul shrinks in isolation.

When you express yourself,
your soul comes out to play.

Self love is more
than a feeling:
it's a sacred ritual.

*You begin by knowing yourself, who you are, now,
today, not who you were before, who you wish you
were, or who others wish you were. You. Today. Now.
Your essence. Your ME.
This is self discovery.*

*As you discover and embrace yourself and your needs,
you begin to care for them. You make time; you make
space. You nurture yourself with your
attention and commitment.
This is self care.*

*You know who you are, and you care for yourself.
All parts of you. The good, the bad, the light, the dark,
the popular, the unpopular, the complex, the simple.
This is self acceptance.*

*You own your worth and fuel it. Your worth is yours.
You are whole, without the infusion of anyone else's
energy, acceptance, love, care, or praise.
This is self worth.*

*And you continue. On and on. Over and over.
You commit to this cycle of self discovery, self care,
self acceptance, and self worth.
This is self love.*

Self care saved my body.
Self love saved my soul.

When I didn't know I was broken,
self care healed me.
When I didn't know I was hiding,
self worth revealed me.
When I didn't know I was growing,
self discovery delighted me.
When I didn't know I was sacred,
self love reminded me.

My daughter's school assignment
was to cast a shadow and
turn it into art.

Maybe that's what
this time is for:
to witness our
shadows and learn
to see their beauty.

How I became whole:

I found my sadness, and loved it.
I found my pain, and loved it.
I found my anger, and loved it.
I found my shame, and loved it.
I found my fear, and loved it.
I found my anxiety, and loved it.

I didn't realize I was homesick
until I came home to myself.

I unknowingly left pieces of myself
behind along the way.
I used to think this meant
I had lost myself.
Now I realize they were crumbs
left behind so I could find my way back
when I was ready to choose myself.

Doing less doesn't
make you worth less.

And if you do less,
everything
will still be okay.

You'll just feel better.

The answer to the questions
you've spent a lifetime asking . . .
will everything be okay,
am I okay, did I do enough,
will it ever be enough, will I feel it,
the happiness, the wholeness, the peace,
the love, the joy, the connection
I so deeply crave?

Yes. If you allow it.

You'll never be enough
as long as you think
soulmates are each
one half of a whole.

I'll love myself whole.
You love yourself whole.
And with all our wholeness,
we will love each other.

Remember when you
thought you couldn't,
and then you did?

Now is the time to
channel that energy.

Inhale:
love, power, worth, hope,
gratitude, grace, trust,
sisterhood, authenticity,
intentionality, truth,
health, intuition,
commitment, delight,
manifestation, kindness,
flexibility, forgiveness,
wholeness, magic, growth,
joy, and peace.

Exhale:
worry, pain, anger, fear,
shame, doubt, resentment,
disappointment, regret,
perfection, isolation,
conflict, chaos, toxins,
negativity, competition,
inflammation, boredom,
guilt, ego, and pressure.

For every time they said
you were too little,
I'm here to tell you
you were and are enough.

For every time they said
you were too much,
I'm here to tell you
you were and are abundant.

*I set out to find
the pot of gold
at the end of the rainbow
and discovered a mirror
instead of a pot.*

Instead of loving people
who withhold their love,
I'm loving myself
and holding space
to receive love from
someone who wants
to give it to me.

I begged for your love.
I bent for your love.
I broke for your love.
And all the while,
all I did,
was beg and bend
and break.

As soon as I remembered
who I am, I forgot
all about you.

I've put you on a hill . . .
more like a mountain.
I've surrounded you with gardens and light
that in the distance shimmering . . .
compel me to climb.
I climb this woman-made incline
this pedestal fueled by the hope . . .
of one day reaching you.
And yet,
the closer I get, the more I realize
each garden is a mirage
created by my love
so determined to find a place
to plant and grow.

I reach you atop my personal Mt. Olympus,
and you stand, and I stand,
and I, no longer craning my neck,
trying to distinguish your glory from
the clouds . . .
realize that sometimes
mountains are really hills
and the glory lies in the climber,
not what awaits at the peak.

Interesting that the
difference between
HOLE and WHOLE
is only one letter.

Maybe it means
our fullness requires that
we embrace our emptiness.

The sun is still the sun
whether it rises or it sets,
and the moon is still the moon
whether it is full or a crescent.

If you love someone,
tell them.
If you're mad at someone,
tell them.
If you miss someone,
tell them.
If you're hurt by someone,
tell them.
If you're thinking about someone,
tell them.
If you need a break from someone,
tell them.
If you're proud of someone,
tell them.
If you need someone,
tell them.

How can I be close to another
if I am not close to myself?

Self love closes the gap between us.

Gratitude means the
glass is always half full
even when there's only
a drop of water left.

Gratitude changes your eyes.
You'll see the good.
Gratitude changes your mouth.
You'll speak the good.
Gratitude changes your hands.
You'll embrace the good.
Gratitude changes your brain.
You'll think the good.
Gratitude changes your heart.
You'll feel the good.
Gratitude changes your energy.
You'll exude the good.

Gratitude changes all of you—you will be the good.

It's often the
quietest voice
in your head
that you need to
listen to the most.

It's still there.
The disappointed voice that says,
"You could have done better."

Only now, there's a softer voice
alongside it that says,
"Hush. She did enough."

When everything feels
like simply too much,
remember this:

there are parts of you
that were designed
to handle precisely
these moments.

She wore her resilience
like a cape,
gossamer made of steel,
translucent yet impenetrable,
its purpose to
both protect and
project her light.

To love yourself is
to come home to yourself.
No matter how far
you've journeyed
or how long you've been away,
you are always
the guest of honor here.
Slip on your crown.
Make a wish on your candles.
The celebration of your
essence starts now.

I climbed inside
the broken doll,
within the broken doll,
within the broken doll,
pulling each apart
until I discovered
my true self,
perfectly intact,
whole, waiting.

I was there all along.

Our light and power
have nothing
to do with the
shape of the bodies
that house us.

Whether she chooses to be full
or chooses to reveal but a sliver,
in plain view or concealed
her light is unquestionable.
She moves persistently,
patiently, consistently,
powerfully.
Waxing or waning,
she illuminates,
a blanket of darkness
no match for her luminosity.
Her dance across the sky an invitation
that electrifies curious souls
and comforts slumbering bodies.
She moves oceans.
She commands tides.
She is the moon.
And she is you.

It's never too late
to reclaim yourself.
Never.

All the parts I had locked away
and neglected are blooming.
I reveal myself to myself
and revel in myself.
Turns out I am not
a tight bud desperately trying
to keep it all together.
I am an open blossom
who is ready to let it all go
and take it all in.

If you're only
earning someone's love
by being less yourself,
you've lost more
than you've gained.

When I was young,
I was lovesick before
I was ever in love.
Everything that followed
required learning that
true love should make
you feel well, not ill.

Judging yourself
is like throwing
down an anchor when
you're trying to swim.

This poem should be better.
I start, I stop.
I try to find the words.
I delete, I pause, I push, I pull.
I end up with nothing more
than this thought:
this poem should be better.
The page empty.
My heart silenced.
This poem should be better.
It should.

Your body hurts when
it's out of alignment.
The same is true
for your soul.

*Self love is
what transforms
your mind, body,
and spirit from
a war zone into
a sanctuary.*

Healing my wounds
instead of hiding them.

The wound,
once omnipotent,
was fraying.
The army of stories it
relied upon no longer
banded together, each one
splintering off and
falling away.
You are weak.
You are worthless.
You are broken.
Each story dissolving into the
well of my self love,
a force that requires no
army to sustain it.

So this is what healing
feels like, I realized.

I pledge allegiance
to the moon,
and to the divine feminine
for which she rises,
one planet under her glow,
indivisible,
with love and light for all.

*I worried myself
into the darkness.*

*I loved myself
into the light.*

When you embrace your true self,
you feel this sense of peace . . .
of not needing to be anything
more than you already are.

The opposite is true
of chasing perfection.
It takes you further
and further away,
while never giving you
an ounce of satisfaction.

So when your head says
seek perfection,

listen to your heart
when it says *be yourself.*

I used to keep a running list
of my imperfections.
A dripping faucet of shame,
that slowly washed me away.

Now I keep a different list.
A running list
of my inherent magic,
that roots me here
and waters me to grow.

The story you
tell yourself
about what happens
is as important
as what happens
to you.

*The whole world feels
whole when I feel whole.
The whole world feels
broken when I feel broken.*

We are mirrors.

Today my therapist said,
"Everyone is doing
their best because no
one wants a bad life,"
and that really
resonated with me.

When the world feels cruel,
be kind to everyone and every thing.

When the world feels out of control,
be patient and take action when you can.

When the world feels dark,
find the light and share it.

When the world feels lost,
be found within yourself
and teach others to do the same.

Have hope,
but do the work.

Trust the universe,
but do the work.

Give it time,
but do the work.

Set intentions,
but do the work.

Believe in magic,
but do the work.

This was it. The reset
she had been waiting for.
But it didn't happen
as she had anticipated.
It wasn't luck or fate or
a gift from the gods.
It wasn't circumstantial.
It wasn't handed down.
It was earned.
A thousand moments of self love
that together formed the mountain
she now stood upon,
as she looked down upon the
valley of opportunity
she was finally ready to claim.

There are 418 million
blades of grass per
person on Earth.

The next time you feel stuck,
remember that like grass,
you too were designed to grow.

A seed doesn't know what lies beyond
its cocoon of dark, warm earth.

It merely honors its intrinsic
desire to grow beyond it.

Self care isn't a threat.
Boundaries aren't rude.
Self love isn't selfish.
Sacrifice isn't feminine.

Read that again.

*On the other side of
consistently practicing
self love and self care
lie new pleasures.*

*The freedom that comes
with setting a boundary.
The fullness that comes
with owning your worth.*

Authenticity fuels fulfillment,
vulnerability fuels connection,
bravery fuels exhilaration,
self love fuels all of the above.

Move as boldly as you feel.
Think as bravely as you dream.
Love as vividly as you fear.
Receive as openly as you give.

To live without purpose
won't kill you,
but you won't truly feel alive.

Your purpose never expires,
no matter how late
you discover or decide to live it.

Your purpose and your day job
don't have to be the same thing.

Living your purpose has intrinsic value,
regardless of external validation
or financial reward.

Once you've discovered your purpose,
you'll know. I promise.

Self discovery inspired the plans.
Self worth poured the foundation.
Self care built the house.
Self love filled the home.

If you love yourself
even half as much
as you loved your crush
in junior high that you
never even spoke to,
you'll be well on your way.

Why does unrequited love linger?
The smell of its hope a stain,
like perfume that remains
even after the laundry.
Why does unrequited love grow
instead of dissipate?
The taste of something you've never had
so vivid on your tongue
it drowns out every other flavor.
Why does unrequited love
cause such prolonged pain?
The phantom tingling of lost limbs
consuming a restless body,
a listless mind, a fervent soul.
Because unrequited love is
the love we owe ourselves.
The intense taste, the touch, the smell . . .
They are your body begging you to
love yourself.

Self Love:

1. You give the gift.
2. You receive the gift.
3. You are the gift.

*When I say
you deserve your own love,
it might seem like
I'm saying you've earned it.*

That's not what I'm saying at all.

*You're entitled to it:
your best, most abundant love.*

*Without lifting a finger.
Without accomplishing one thing.
Without being or doing a drop
more than the day you were born.*

Love is ~~blind.~~

seeing everything and choosing
someone for everything they are.

When I choose my forever love,
I will say that it was love at last sight.
That the love we shared early on continued to grow
based on every interaction, every experience, every
time something new was shared between us.

One day, I will toast the fact that the love that got us
down the aisle was based on everything that came after
"first sight," like learning about each other's
authentic selves, strengths, and even weaknesses.

That the love was not because of some instant gut
feeling but because every day, every time we said
goodbye, we could honestly say we experienced a new,
more meaningful love . . . at each last sight.

Self love is
the foundation
of all love.

Modern love isn't give and take.
Modern love is release and receive.
Release what stands in the way of love,
and receive the love that is shared.
No expectations. No demands.
No barriers. No disappointment.
Only mutual surrender.
Only abundant love.

Self care: the radical notion
you deserve your own attention.

Today is anything
you need it to be.
A slow day of rest in
the middle of the week.
The first day of the
rest of your life.
The end.
The beginning.
Action. Silence.
Just another day,
or THE day.
Whatever it is:
make it yours.

The only way to get
what you want
is to know what that is.

I desire to feel alive in every moment.
To feel the push and pull of electricity
that connects everyone and everything.
To know what I want, and to want it not just
intellectually but with every cell in my body.
To feel it vibrating and radiating, inch by inch,
until it energizes the very well of my being.
More than anything, I want this desire to pulse
through me toward the people I love.
So we can feel so close our hearts beat in unison.

Self love and sisterhood
will save the planet.

A woman who embraces her history.
A woman who charts her path.
A woman who honors her needs.
A woman who speaks her truth.
A woman who shines her light.
A woman who celebrates her sisters.

This is what it means to be a woman
who chooses herself.

Dear sister,

I know that today, and many
days right now, are scary,
uncertain, dark. But your light
gives me hope, and together
we will remind the world that
humanity is intact and
love will prevail.

*If the sun still rises
and the moon still glows
and the tides still rush
forward and back
and the bees still hum
and the earth still blooms
and the wind still gently
kisses your cheeks,
then there are still
reasons to be grateful.*

ABOUT THE AUTHOR

Melody Godfred is the Self Love Philosopher. As a poet, author, and entrepreneur, she is devoted to empowering people to love themselves and transform their lives. She is the founder of the global self love movement Fred and Far and creator of the Self Love Pinky Ring™. Her poetry has been featured by Oprah Daily *and* TODAY *with Hoda & Jenna, among others, for its wisdom and ability to deeply resonate and uplift.*

Melody lives in Los Angeles with the love of her life, Aaron; twins, Stella and Violet; and son, Teddy. Learn more at melodygodfred.com and fredandfar.com and connect with her @melodygodfred and @fredandfar.